Felt This so Many Times

Poems by Antony V. Plocido

Kansas City　　　　Missouri

Spartan Press
Kansas City, Missouri
spartanpresskc.com

Copyright (c) Tony Plocido, 2018
First Edition 1 3 5 7 9 10 8 6 4 2
ISBN: 978-1-946642-52-3
LCCN: 2018943071

Design, edits and layout: Tony Plocido, Missi Rasmussen, Jason Ryberg
Cover image: Tony Plocido
Author photo: Tony Plocido
All rights reserved. No part of this publication may be reproduced or transmitted in any form or by any means, electronic or mechanical, including photocopying, recording or by info retrieval system, without prior written permission from the author.

Felt This so Many Times

Poems by Antony V. Plocido

Kansas City   Missouri

Spartan Press
Kansas City, Missouri
spartanpresskc.com

Copyright (c) Tony Plocido, 2018
First Edition 1 3 5 7 9 10 8 6 4 2
ISBN: 978-1-946642-52-3
LCCN: 2018943071

Design, edits and layout: Tony Plocido, Missi Rasmussen, Jason Ryberg
Cover image: Tony Plocido
Author photo: Tony Plocido
All rights reserved. No part of this publication may be reproduced or transmitted in any form or by any means, electronic or mechanical, including photocopying, recording or by info retrieval system, without prior written permission from the author.

Spartan Press would like to thank Prospero's Books, The Fellowship of N-finite Jest, The Prospero Institute of Disquieted P/o/e/t/i/c/s, Will Leathem, Tom Wayne, Jeanette Powers, j. d. tulloch, Jon Bidwell, Jason Preu, Mark McClane, Tony Hayden and the whole Osage Arts Community.

This book couldn't have been possible without the love, support, and/or opportunity provided by the following people:

Jason Ryberg – I tried to give the book back and he wouldn't take it. Thanks for believing in me.

Amy Koz Marvel – For being a longtime friend and collaborator. She's not in this book (she was in the last book) but she's an artistic motivator. She's an absolute painter with words. @amykaypoetry (Instagram)

Rana Clack (Martin) – Your love and belief in me, during this time period (and any future time periods), means the world to me.

The entire **Prospero's Books** (KC) Family - Will, Tom, Jason (again), and the rest. You gave me the launch pad to really start believing in myself as a writer. I will never forget you for that.

Eat My Words Bookstore / Scott VanKoughnett (MN) – Scott, thank you so much for carrying my books in your store, for believing me as a poet, and for all of the wonderful chats. You're a true patron of the arts.

David Bayliss – For letting me in on your pet project, Poets and Pints, and for believing in my work.

Missi Rasmussen – Thank you for being a friend (proceed to sing the Golden Girls theme). Thank you for being my editor.

Jennifer Pendarvis – I didn't end up using your cover art but I thank you for taking the time to consider it. I appreciate your vision and your art.

My mom, dad, brothers Jason and Nathan, sister Samantha, step-parents Prudence and Bill, and all my friends who continue to support me. Continue to love me.

-Tony Plocido

CONTENTS

If I could just go back to June of 1994 / 1

Gram / 4

Felt This So Many Times / 6

Let Me Tell You What I'm Not / 7

Argument II (When we're Sober) / 9

…at the Table / 12

The Stew Would be Different / 14

Living in the Dawn
 (Oh They're Just Trying to Help, Right?) / 16

Distancing the Divine / 18

Recall / 20

Some Social / 22

Tour Bus / 24

I Really Shouldn't / 26

Time isn't Passive / 28

The Freedom Party
 (It's Going to be a Fabulous Affair) / 31

Thoughts on Topography / 33

Expense / 35

42 and Something New / 37

Me and What I Want / 39

Usquebaugh / 42

More Like Jane / 44

That Thing at the Top of the Cabinet / 46

You're the Last Thing / 47

You May Not Understand / 49

Expiration / 51

Standing in the Doorway / 53

Fairy Tales / 56

Cold Wit(H)er / 57

If I Failed You / 59

The Ghosts of My Gender / 61

Still I Made It / 63

Felt This So Many Times

If I Could Just Go Back to June of 1994 (Prologue)

Fresh out of high school (where I didn't try) but before paying for college (where I didn't try).

If I could back there, I wouldn't have smoked that first bowl. I wouldn't have stuck out my tongue for that first stamp. I wouldn't have stuck my fingers, in a bag, for that first fungus, or drank Busch Light ever.

How are the memories, where my mind was so clouded, so crystal clear?

I remember the path, I was walking, the first time that smoke hit my throat and made me cough until I sat down. The creep feeling coming over the crown of head as my crimson eyes slanted down.

I remember the entire day after. The sun was at my nine in the woods where everything was suddenly hilarious. Then hunger became my only engine. Poor choice for the fat kid.

I remember the din of the batting cages thirty minutes after the paper dissolved. It was all too much. I needed fresh air. I needed open space. I remember sitting on the curb as the shadows danced and bent to unheard rhythms and breath. I remember trespassing. The dark tunnels and workers all were eluded.

We were the night, that night. I remember how Phish controlled my ears. As eight or so hours flittered away. I remember finally laying down and only seeing faces as they flew at me. The only remedy was the lights.

I remember we brewed the fungus. Broke it down like Oolong with a process so intricate and precise that one had to write it down first. These dark pre-Google days, as the clock ticked by an hour, tea was served.

We all scalded our throats trying to take it in as quick is possible. We wanted the ride to start and temperature was not going to be a governor. As the wave washed in, I sat with crayons and giant sheet of paper. I proceeded to draw a tornado for about 3 and half hours. The sounds of Native Americans chanting on a cassette. We took turns flipping the tape. There would be no other music. There was no need.

I couldn't be more clear about these experiences if I had a video. They shine in my head.

But…

I don't remember her last name. The first girl, that ever gave herself to me. Christ, we dated! It wasn't a one-night stand. I can't remember her name or face. Or the second one. I don't remember learning how to read, learning math, or even how to swim. These are just assumptions at this point. I don't know how so many years have gone by since then. I think I've missed.

I think that I was the target watching as the arrow
sailed wide. Why wasn't the future important?
Why is it now? Is it really as simple as getting old?

I don't accept that. My logic-leaning mind won't
accept my lack of anticipation. My lack of participation.
My lack of perspiration. My lack of aspirations.
It needs definition.

Gram

The sounds of family
was the only peace she needed.
A crossword and
a visiting neighbor
brought on a joy
that was passed into her food.
Though
she would complain
about both right after.

Her view was that of wife and
mother and
grandmother.
She made sure I felt love
in a family
where I often felt foreign.

We passed so much time
together.

But life is a light and
all light fades.
The result isn't darkness.
It's space.

Space we don't know
what to do with.

For now
I am storing my memories there.

Aspetta tu
Just you wait
Once was her warning.
Now, a promise for the future.

~for Rose Plocido. Gram. 1925-2017

Felt This So Many Times

My face has been scarred with disappointment and
>*shame, - I've*

felt this so many
>*times - I've*

wanted to say I'm sorry to
>*you - wouldn't*

listen anyway.   I'm the monster that
>*kills - me*

how we stopped talking.   We were something
>*big - isn't*

the type of gesture I would need
>*now - I*

just want a soft
>*touch - me.*

Maybe somewhere that I forgot existed.
Somewhere deep in the memories I thought
>*I made-up - these*

moments of reconciliation to ease sadness.
This way I wouldn't get
>*scars - on my face*

are from disappointment.

I really should have seen you coming.

Let Me Tell You What I'm Not

I wasn't a fully formed human
when I last spoke your name.
I was half the size
of the words you used
to berate me.
The slings and arrows had
Shakespearian perfection.
I just wished
we could have danced
in silence
a bit longer.
The air was not full
of misunderstanding.
We could breathe
in a way that didn't hurt.

I have grown some.

Being a man
has no real meaning to me. But
I have grown.
I know
now
that I am not those flaws
in your lenses.

You
are not those monsters
that I fed.
We are just people.

Broken, stupid,
beautiful, intelligent
people.

We seek unicorns
but can only find horses.

Argument II
(When we're Sober)

There is a moment where I explode.
I tried to hold it all in
but you wouldn't listen
when I asked for quiet.
I wasn't ready for a riot.
I need conversation.
This is confrontation and
I'm trying to gather up my insides.
You ride a tide of blind faith
that you're inexorably right.
Truth with savagery.
An excuse to battle me. And
I haven't said a god damned thing!

But now the words pour.
They're powder in a fan.
You try to stand clear but
there's no way out of here.
Remember when peer pressure
was your biggest problem?
Now in the autumn of your life
you've come across me.
Once a pillar of patience.
A saint since the fourth grade.

But you've made a demon.
Yelling and screaming,
your scheming and plotting.
Not dotting your "*I*"s,
unfinished letters and lies. And
I'm barely even tired.

So now I have my gloves on.
My trunks on. The audience is rabid.
Your words vapid and yet you dance.
You attempt an *Ali* stance.
You say you're the greatest.
Your latest attempt to be significant.
In this present tense,
I'm not feeling it.
Pretty sure you were better in the past.
So we're going to go rounds.
You pound then I pound and
the sound is a terrific definition
of a nonsensical division of similar ideas.
Christ, we aren't even listening to each other!

When we separate, a bell
reverberates in my head.
I'm just dead. Done with this bray.
Why don't we say what we mean?
It's a simple concept.
Cool and clean.   But
we don't do it.

We blow through it. Intent.
Content. And only find
dissent.   It's silly.
We're left with me and you,
standing in a room
surrounded by our muses,
with fresh bumps and bruises.
Trying to apologize for a problem
that never really existed.

…at the Table

1.
She speaks of
windows, souls, and
how to see through the bars.

She speaks of
injuries, surgeries, and
how to lighten the scars.

She speaks of
communication, fornication, and
what's missing in life.

She speaks of
respect, neglect, and
her asking twice.

She speaks of
mountains and how then
are we supposed to make it.

She speaks of
laughter and after
we no longer take it.

2.
I listened.
Face granite
glistened with tears.
She hears
my thoughts. I'm caught.
They are perceptible.
They aren't acceptable.
They sink me.
She thinks me cold.
She thinks me callus.
She thinks too much. And
as the hush of facts
settle in the cracks
of this room,
I feel her loom
behind me.

She reminds me
that this shouldn't be a surprise.
Everyday,
every
single
day,
I choose to be alive.

Fuck. She's right.

The Stew Would be Different

I remember
when I couldn't remember.
When the room smelled
like old grass and
I was never going to be a human.
The haze played well
with the battle of self-worth.

Low thoughts are often overlooked.

Comedy happens.
Laughter propels beyond
anything of sense.
Simple looks become
the best joke every told.
Breath becomes short yet
I continue to inhale.

There is always a moment
when the joke leaves the room.

Then it's all stares and hunger.
The foods consumed
had the nutritional value of a beach ball.
Also, the *gateway* label
isn't a complete fallacy.

I had journeys and
I did far more damage to my heart
than my lungs.

In more ways than I can count.

I want to say
that I shouldn't have put it
on my tongue.
That I shouldn't have put her
on my tongue.
I shouldn't have explored
the dark rooms in my head.
I want to say this.

Every action is an ingredient.
You take one away and
everything is different.

I wouldn't be comfortable with that, either.

Living in the Dawn
(Oh, they are only trying to help. Right?)

Sadness,
like the dawn,
is easier to detect the beginning
then to determine the end.

Advice continues to intersect,
perpendicular in its approach,
emotional stoplights would be good;
because I don't want to keep crashing.

I stand holding my own hands
wishing for a sudden departure.
Not of self but of the sullen mood.

I release my meal
stand and feel
the same.

Tears drip on
like the faucet
I've been meaning to fix.
Shit! I wish I would have done that.

I pace a divot in the flooring
as friends, *friends,* and family
spew their thoughts on my existence.

My head bends back
at the power they believe me to have.
I feel bad that I haven't saved a life
or defeated a dictator
with all this untapped potential.
It's funny how weak I feel
after these exchanges.

They tell me it will work out.
They tell me it will work.
They tell me I will be better.

But every thought I have
makes me feel closer to the dawn
but not close enough to the day.

Distancing the Divine

I don't believe in anything I can't touch.
It's not much to think that life
is an accident.
I know you want providence.
You want a sense knowing you aren't entirely
responsible.

I can pull facts and figures.
Create cracks and fissures in your argument. But
nothing will dent your resolve.
You will keep hearing voices from hidden things.
It takes the sting out of being alone.

I've prayed too many times
to blind minds and deaf ears.
Shed tears for lost causes and
caused losses.
I spent a lot of youth hoping
divinity would boost my current situation
just to the level of livable.
I felt I was forgivable.
My transgressions were part
of life lessons and I was mostly
on the sincere side of *sorry.* But
he…or she…didn't hear me.

So, in the present tense
I seek evidence and I don't feel the least
like I'm wrong.
Don't feel the least attached
to the song.

If there is a plan
in the bland life that I've lived,
it's full of falling walls,
dead-end halls and
countless mistakes to forgive.

Any other architect would be fired for that.

Recall

I don't remember learning how to read.
I don't recall when words
clicked into sentences.
When nouns differentiated themselves
from verbs.

I don't remember love songs.
Not by heart. And
yet they are on repeat,
in my head,
through the times I'm not with you.

I don't remember what *home* means.
I'm never comfortable.
I have a bed made of heaven and
sleep eludes.
I toss until I become dizzy enough to pass out.

I don't remember your name.
You don't exist but
I had named you. All of you.
My immortality.
The day will come when my imprint has lifted.

I don't remember how to deal with this.

My bucket list exists but
it's written on mile signs
beyond the horizon.

The journey will take the rest of my time.

Some Social

We are roman candles.
Attention welcomed.
We shine bright
then
inevitably
burn out.

We can feel desolation
even in a crowded room.
The bold-hearted introverts
who shine,
then dim as we saunter home.

The long goodbye
is torture.
We'd rather find the bathroom and
then find the door.

Battery drained.

We seek solace.
Silence.
Not sentiment.

In these moments

we can't remember
the invite.
The drive to go.
We can't remember
how to be surrounded
by faces.

We don't feel shame,
in this life,
for this behavior.

Our string can be pulled,
but eventually
the movement stops.

Tour Bus

There isn't time anymore.
My calendar has requirements.
My girlfriend has needs.
My work wants a third of my life.
There isn't time.

However, in the times
when I had more time,
I wished I had less.
The day wouldn't work towards its end
like it's supposed to.
It would stretch and pull.
A sort of taffy.
We're never really satisfied with taffy.

Sometimes I think
it's good we forget.
Total recall would break me.
I have lingered
in unimaginably mundane moments.
So much sloth.
So many poems I didn't write.

I feel like this let so many people
off the hook.

Their misdeeds won't get observed.
Pointed out.
Time
is the tour bus
not the driver.
It will never care
if you can see clearly.

I Really Shouldn't

The sunlight paints you a different color
from the night stained blue,
that entered my room last night.
The scent of sex,
which lingered like fog
as we passed out,
is now just a distant hint.
Barely noticeable.

Bare skin
shines against the dark blue sheets.
You're twisted in them.
I follow the contortions.

You sleep.
You breathe. And
I think
Our lives have just begun.

I hope you're dreaming about dogs.
I hate dogs but
you love them and
I think that I want breakfast.

I want to make you eggs
on every day
that ends in day.

Because I love eggs and
you love
satisfaction.

You take a deep breath and
you rotate.
Now I can see the remnants
of the burgundy lipstick
that so tangoed with my psyche.

You'll wake soon.
I'm sure you'll tear through this fantasy.
A hurricane of reality and
I never think I should board up the windows.

For now,
you're eternity that I can touch.
I have named our children.
I have figured out where we'll retire.
I ignore the clock on the wall.

Then you wake,
stretch,
smile awkwardly.
You dress and decline my eggs.
The door closes and
all of the cards
fall to the floor.

Time isn't Passive
(for Bill P.)

Last night
my dream ended with me
getting shot in the chest
the rest
is a blur. Just a mixture
of shapes and sounds.
All ground down
to a shot in the chest.

To the best
of my knowledge
I was not dead.
Instead,
I woke the next day
to texts saying my friend
was in a coma.
Fell off a ladder.
Hurt his bladder or spleen
or something in between
and I was shook.

I never took kindly
to people who blindly interpret dreams.
They tell you what it means
when XYZ happens.

I always think,
How could you know?
But when I woke up slow,
with a hand on my heart,
I didn't part with the dismay.
I thought I might have been sick.

And this
was no news for a Monday.
Or any day that ends in *day*.
When your brother's in trouble,
you double the panic.
Your mind is not
subtle or static.
You have no rope to fling him.
Nothing that will bring him
to consciousness.
And it's not just this
that bothers you.

Nobody's ever said
ALL they need to say to a person.
One diversion or another
pushes you further into
forgetfulness.
Then regretfulness.

Time isn't passive.
Suddenly there's a massive
bucket list undone.
A *Fuck it* list unsung. And
no one knows how you feel.
Suddenly it's all so real.

We're always searching for a moral.

The Freedom Party
(It's Going to be a Fabulous Affair)

For food,
it's pot luck
You're free to feast
on shitty tweets
or snicker salad.
It's all here.

For cocktails,
along with martinis, cosmos, or mimosa,
we also have a clumpy
viscous substance
that tastes like shame.
We call it
The Texas Voting Laws.

For music,
(You're gonna love this)
we have Lee Greenwood
doing Bruce Springsteen's cover
of American Woman (by the Guess Who)
while jerking off into an American flag.
Because the material is soft and
also, we love Canada.

You are allowed to pick
from two dances.
Square or
Line.
Because we aren't really sure
if we should have a partner.

So please,
enjoy this Freedom Party
because the poor paid for it.
Rich, white folks love it.
And we wouldn't want
to let either of them down.

Thoughts on Topography

A delicious silence
between each of the breaths.
Her chest rose and fell
in time with the tide.
Her skin matched the sand.
Almost invisible from here.

The air smelled spoiled and
salty.
The sun was saying its goodbyes.
I had forgotten what brought me here.
Thoughts for her had become strong.
Strong like whiskey or
a hurricane.
I felt drunk and boarded.

Yet, everything was still.
Completely.
Except her chest.
The topography of her torso
would have made a lesser man cry.

In the stillness
I could hear the last song to touch my ears.
It wasn't happy and
it was a poor soundtrack to this movie.
I could feel the dénouement approaching.

I walk over.
Look down
as the sun ticks shadows across her body.
I wondered if
she wondered anything at all.
She's a museum piece.
There was no touching. No photography.

Poets speak of beauty
in the moments between moments.
In that instance
I finally understood.

Expense

I am one of those people that
always has five things in his pocket.
Eh, sometimes it's just
two or three.
The point is
I'm always carrying weight.
The weight
of things
I'm never going to need.

Sometimes it's Chapstick and
sometimes it's an overwhelming desire to flee.
Sometimes it's $.35 and
sometimes it's an anger at always being the fat kid.
Sometimes
it's just a note to myself
telling me, *forget you ever knew her.*

Every day, I shake it off.
I say things like,
You've made this far, dummy.
Why not keep walking?
or
Buy that sandwich.
The cost is minimal
compared to the joy you'll feel.

I can't help but think
that all of this talk
comes at an expense.
Eventually the window will break
even if you're only throwing
the tiniest of pebble.

I have to be ready to answer the question,
What if all the costs are real?

42 and Something New

I started
as an observer to a war.
A silent war.
A cold war.
They loved only emptiness
for too many years.
I really didn't mean to get involved.
A friend.
That was my role.

But when someone
leans on you long enough,
you will eventually fall.
We both fell.
We crashed…hard.

Now all my thoughts
are extended into the future.
All my thoughts
are filled with forever.
Forever was always tricky for me.
I mean it's a destination
you can't ever reach.
It's never forever.
The ultimate carrot on a stick.

I have stayed out of it but
I am in it.
I fill her head with happiness and
I feel something new.

42 years old and
I feel something new.

I don't envy the road she travels.
It's bumpy road to my doorstep.
All others have turned around.
She seems determined.
I wish her all the strength in the world.

Me and What I Want

I, sometimes, see your face
in the empty chairs
at my table.
Sometimes smiling.
Sometimes crying.
Sometimes screaming.
It's a torrid scene,
regardless of mood.

Your small hands reach for me.
They are open,
ready for substance.
My heart hurts
from the distance.

This world is so God damned mean.

There is a special kind of darkness
without you.
The light has always
cast weird shadows.
Dark shapes of unfamiliarity
create paths to incorrect locations.

I can only assume
you have the same problem.

This would explain your absence.
This would explain why after 25 years,
of praying for you,
you still have not arrived.

I've wanted,
I mean really wanted,
three things in this life.
A job I can respect.
A person to love. And
you,
my child.

There is so much selfishness
in that want.
It's better to get what you need. And
I need to be less selfish.
I need to find improvement. Not
a blank slate,
to transfer on to,
my undying opinions.

This is the reality
of why sought being a dad.
Another me.
Immortality.
All these thoughts
had no visions of your mother.

Just me.

Me.

Me.

It doesn't change the fact,
that on occasion,
I see you reach for me.
Smile at me.
Scream at me.

Me!

Me!

Well, little one,
we'll live better apart.
Where I can control my life and
you can have yours.

But I will continue to reach for you
in my thoughts.
Because ultimately I,
like everyone else,
am dying.
This sentence is almost over.

You were my chance for another paragraph.

Usquebaugh

Usquebaugh
liquid, brown
love
water of life.
You rest my soul
when the world tries
too
hard.
You make heads hard
and groins soft.
You make idiots
out of masters.

You're measured in fingers and
you wrap your hands around me.
Your burn doesn't add fear
it adds texture and
I hold you.

Close.

Close like the distance of my tongue
to my lips and
I sip
slowly.

Urgency
is an insult.
Savor.
My thoughts only wrap around this idea.

When I feel down.
Dead.
It's usquebaugh.
Whiskey.

The Water of Life.

More Like Jane

I wish I knew love
like I know the concept.
I wish love had touched me
the way my pen had touched it.
I wish it could stand before the world and
describe my importance.

It could explain
how I am closer than I appear.
It could martyr itself before me
as I stand there
like the distinguished gent
in a Jane Austen novel.

Instead, I sit here
more like Jane.

These are not proper thoughts for a man.
Not in her time
nor in mine.
These are the mindlings of children.

Love is not a character in a story.
It is a reason for the page.
It is the inevitable result
of the ink.

It's much like a storm.
It has its beauty.
Destruction
It never tires.

Unlike myself.

I have tired a thousand times over and
still I sit at this desk,
searching.

That Thing at the Top of the Cabinet

In the days of douchey, yellow-faced,
tyrant-asaurus Frump…

We see people's skeletons
rising
like it was only normality
keeping them in the ground.
We see their sense of decency
was just a shirt they wore
to blend in.

We live in a time
where we have to be told
that black lives matter,
that Nazis are bad, and
that women are equal.

There had been a wave
carrying the oppressed,
discriminated against, and
a beacon of progress.
It was bringing them all
to shore.

Now it seems the earth
has shifted.
The future is the past. And
we still have three more years.

You're the Last Thing

There's a whole world outside.
I get told this in countless languages.

There's a whole universe inside.
I get told this every time I just — can't.

I don't,
immediately,
have sadness for you.
Empathy is important
but not imbedded.

I have to find it.
Like the way you find your smile
when I approach.
It's not instant.
Ready.

Find it I do.
Always.
Eternally.

I would do anything for you.
Even if,
I can't do anything with you.

I would feel anything with you
Even if,
I can't do anything to you.

You're the last thing
I will hold on to
as lights start to dim and
the floor falls out.

I know this because
the lights aren't on now and
I can only see your face.

You May Not Understand

I stand twisting in (what I consider)
prophetic ramblings.

Everybody hears me.
No one is listening.

If I told you that God spoke to me,
(He hasn't)
You would nod and agree
because belief dictates that you do.

I haven't heard his voice
but he speaks to me none-the-less,
through challenges laid upon me.

I look back and
almost lose my stomach over it.
I am constantly telling God (and you)
You know it wasn't fair.
All the roads you laid before me,
without signs.
It wasn't fair to make ME choose.

Which is bullshit.

All of it.

I mean the decision has to be mine
otherwise I can only resent the outcome.

God is a funny thing.
All things that keep life going are funny things.
Water, air, bacteria, nutrients.
None of them, you can wrap your hands around,
yet we all accept them as real.
Hell, water is the only one we can even see.
I stay comfortable knowing
there is a tremendous amount of acceptance in life.

Expiration

As we laid talking,
baby sleeping a breath away,
the moment arrived.
There was months
worth of chatter
that lead to this moment.

My drink set down
on the night stand.
I turned your way.
Your eyes made me
feel like a child
on Christmas morning.
That moment you realize
you don't have to wonder
anymore.
Your gifts are at hand.

I took a moment to
touch your hair.
I touched my nose
to yours.
Distance erased.
Breath being shared.
Lips danced.

This kiss had
fireworks,
it had
magic,
it had
an expiration date.

I am not sure how much time passed
that evening; but
I know how much has passed, since.

I just know that night
I wasn't steering
or thinking.
I was simply funneled
by life
or God
or love
to that spot.

I write poems
because of spots like that.

Standing in the Doorway

So here we are.
No flames to fan and
the cold night is setting in.
Our belongings are spliced together.
Wires.
The cables that use to conduct
this electricity are now
being divided. Frayed.
There are sparks but
not of celebration.

I used to celebrate my memories of you.
I thought I was
all in.
I thought I was
just you.
I thought I was
done worrying about tomorrow.
I shouldn't think so much.
It means I'm not paying attention.

But I've paid for your attention.
I have $10.00 left,
my tank is empty, and
I need bread.

I feel sandwiched between
your need to participate and
your need to evacuate.
The *in* door and the *out* door
are the same door.
It comes down to your orientation.

I went to orientation for
the School of You.
I studied the syllabus,
mapped my classes, but
my grades left something
to be desired.
Too much time in detention.
I made the mistake
of being your class clown.
But you can't fuck funny.

So funny is what fucked me.
But when you would giggle
my insides would melt.
I felt that laughter
as oxygen.
Breathing it in would
make me dizzy.
I would fall,
look up and
find you've had enough.

Enough time has passed.
We tried to pull the cord,
over and over,
the engine wouldn't start.
Again.
We can't live life
parked in the shed. Dead.
So here we are.
Saying I love you
for the last time.

Fairy Tales

I want a lasting relationship
with my country.
I want to feel like patriotism
is important.
I want to know
that everyone is ok where they are.
I want to see beauty
in every direction I look.

Even down.

I want to hear
the soft sigh of relief
as the people finally stand up.

It turns out that magic isn't real.

Cold Wit(H)er

I went outside.
The snow had silenced everything.
The cars, the birds,
the magic.
This is why the crunch,
under my feet,
was so loud.
There was no stealth
in my approach.

She looked dead,
lying in the snow, with her eyes closed.
The temperature had to look up
to see zero and
she says,
It's not cold.
It's invigorating.

And I thought,
It can't be both?
I am glad I didn't say that out loud.
She's having a moment and
I've ruined so many of them.

Her teeth are chattering.
Mind gone. (just my opinion)
It's easy to make snap judgments
when your body has slowed.
From the cold
or from bad decisions.
She says to follow.

I won't.
I'm pulled sideways,
then back.
Never towards.
I want warmth and
her.
Apparently, I can't have both.

If I Failed You

If I failed you
in some manner,
I don't remember
or the days were wrong.
The moon was in the wrong house.
It was probably a Saturday.

I tend lose track of Saturdays.

If I failed you
in some manner,
did I say I was sorry?
Did you tell me I need to?
I am not always aware.
My eyes are open
but the visions of bright ideas
can block my view.

I never know when this will happen.

If I failed you
in some manner,
it's because you expected me not to.
I plant and grow expectations
as much as you.

Sometimes things die.
Balls get dropped.

This is tough because
I was hungry for it too.

Let us feast on forgiveness instead.

The Ghosts of My Gender

All she's got is long hair and
ghosts from her past.
The brume of hosts from her wild life.
The flume of smoke
from the fire light
inside her contempt.
I've spent many a thought
figuring how I ought to
bring down the temperature.
How I ought to
swing round and comfort her. But

I'm too similar.
Because to her I am

another bearded face.
Another crime scene.

Though my fashion is
of a gentler sort,
there is no solid retort for this.

I can't undo the knots
of shame and vulnerability.
The blame isn't on me
but I stand-in.

I feel abandoned by my gender.
I have surrendered
to their crimes. And
my mind drifts too far away.

No, she won't stay.
We'll play this co-dependence game
until the suspense wears off.
Until the high starts to drop.
Then we'll walk in separate directions.

The ghosts
will continue to follow her.

Still I Made it

If my teachers had guns
they would have shot me first.
I was the antithesis
of what they wanted.
The smart kid
who didn't want to learn.
Aerosolized potential
destroying their ozone layer.
I was the proverbial millennial
on the wrong side of 2000.

Antony V. Plocido (Tony) was born in Minneapolis, MN. He's been writing poetry since he was a child. In 2011, he decided to move to Kansas City to further expand his poetry. He published his first book, *Sucker Punch Wisdom* (Write the Future Press), with two other Kansas City poets, Jeremy O'Neal & William Peck on Halloween, 2012. He has since moved back to the Twin Cities in Minnesota and released his second book, *Aging and Other Side Projects,* in December 2016. Tony continues to be the webmaster for the Poets & Pints series in Minneapolis (3rd Wed). He has an old cat which is probably a metaphor but he doesn't know for what. You can reach him at www.mentalvalley.com.

This project was made possible, in part, by generous support from the Osage Arts Community.

Osage Arts Community provides temporary time, space and support for the creation of new artistic works in a retreat format, serving creative people of all kinds — visual artists, composers, poets, fiction and nonfiction writers. Located on a 152-acre farm in an isolated rural mountainside setting in Central Missouri and bordered by ¾ of a mile of the Gasconade River, OAC provides residencies to those working alone, as well as welcoming collaborative teams, offering living space and workspace in a country environment to emerging and mid-career artists. For more information, visit us at www.osageac.org

Osage Arts Community

www.ingramcontent.com/pod-product-compliance
Lightning Source LLC
Chambersburg PA
CBHW021449080526
44588CB00009B/769